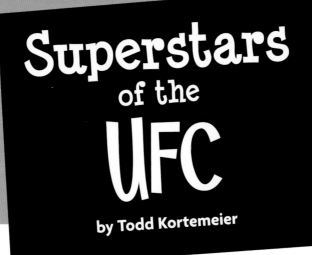

Superstars
of the
UFC

by Todd Kortemeier

AMICUS HIGH INTEREST • AMICUS INK

Amicus High Interest and Amicus Ink
are imprints of Amicus
P.O. Box 1329, Mankato, MN 56002
www.amicuspublishing.us

Library of Congress Cataloging-in-Publication Data
Names: Kortemeier, Todd, 1986- author.
Title: Superstars of the UFC / by Todd Kortemeier.
Other titles: Superstars of the Ultimate Fighting Championship
Description: Mankato, MN : Amicus High Interest, [2016] | Series: Pro
sports superstars | Includes index.
Identifiers: LCCN 2015033456 (print) | LCCN 2016004265 (ebook) |
  ISBN 9781607539391 (hardcover)
  ISBN 9781681510293 (pdf ebook)
  ISBN 9781681521046 (paperback)
Subjects: LCSH: Mixed martial arts--Juvenile literature. | Martial artists--
Biography--Juvenile literature. | UFC (Mixed martial arts event)--Juvenile
literature.
Classification: LCC GV1102.7.M59 K67 2016 (print) | LCC GV1102.7.M59
(ebook)| DDC 796.80922--dc23
LC record available at http://lccn.loc.gov/2015033456

Photo Credits: Isaac Brekken/AP Images, cover, 6; Eric Jamison/AP Images,
2, 14–15; David Becker/AP Images, 5, 18–19, 22; Jae C. Hong/AP Images,
8–9, 16; AP Images, 10–11; Julie Jacobson/AP Images, 12; John Locher/AP
Images, 20–21

Produced for Amicus by The Peterson Publishing Company
and Red Line Editorial.

Editor Arnold Ringstad
Designer Becky Daum

Printed in the United States of America
North Mankato, MN

HC 10 9 8 7 6 5 4 3 2 1
PB 10 9 8 7 6 5 4 3 2 1

TABLE OF CONTENTS

ULTIMATE FIGHTERS

UFC stands for Ultimate Fighting Championship. Fighters use **mixed martial arts**. They hit big. They kick hard. Fights last up to five rounds. Each round is five minutes. There are many UFC stars. Here are some of the best.

5

RANDY COUTURE

Randy Couture was an early star. His first fight was in 1997. He won in the first round. He was great at taking fighters down. He won the **heavyweight title** three times.

Couture later became a movie star.

CHUCK LIDDELL

Chuck Liddell was a strong fighter. He was hard to knock out. He won his first fight in 1998. He held the **light heavyweight** title for two years.

ANDERSON SILVA

Anderson Silva joined the UFC in 2006. He is very fast. His nickname is "the Spider." His fights don't last long. Only five have gone past two rounds.

Silva has the longest winning streak. He won 16 fights in a row.

CAIN VELASQUEZ

Cain Velasquez is a top heavyweight fighter. He won his first title in 2010. He won another in 2012. He hits with a lot of power. Most of his fights end in the first round.

Velasquez was a wrestler in college.

JOSÉ ALDO

José Aldo held the **featherweight** title from 2011 to 2015. He defended it seven times. Aldo is fast. He punches hard. It isn't easy to bring him down.

RONDA ROUSEY

Ronda Rousey is one of the best female UFC fighters. She won the first women's UFC title in 2013. It was over in round one. She won a 2015 fight in only 14 seconds. Rousey uses **judo**.

CHRIS WEIDMAN

Chris Weidman won the **middleweight** title in 2013. He beat Anderson Silva. Weidman is good at taking down fighters. He hits hard. Many of his fights end in **knockouts**.

McGregor once worked as a plumber.

CONOR McGREGOR

Conor McGregor joined the UFC in 2013. He kicks hard. By 2015 he had 17 knockouts. He is one of the UFC's rising stars.

The UFC has had many great superstars. Who will be next?

UFC FAST FACTS

Founded: 1993

Headquarters: Las Vegas, Nevada

Major Events Held: 194 through 2015

Most Title Defenses: 10, Anderson Silva

Most Title Fights: 15, Randy Couture

Countries to Host Events: 10

Weight Classes: Eight men's classes and two women's classes

Fight Length: Three five-minute rounds for non-championship fights, five five-minute rounds for championship fights

WORDS TO KNOW

featherweight – a fighter weighing between 135 and 145 pounds

heavyweight – a fighter weighing between 205 and 265 pounds

judo – a Japanese fighting style that involves throws and holds

knockout – when a fight ends before the scheduled time because one fighter is unable to continue

light heavyweight – a fighter weighing between 185 and 205 pounds

middleweight – a fighter weighing between 170 and 185 pounds

mixed martial arts – a type of fighting competition that includes many fighting styles

title – a championship victory within a UFC weight class

LEARN MORE

Books

Castellano, Peter. *MMA*. New York: Gareth Stevens, 2015.

Jones, Patrick. *Ultimate Fighting: The Brains and Brawn of Mixed Martial Arts*. Minneapolis, MN: Millbrook Press, 2014.

Websites

ESPN: MMA

http://espn.go.com/mma

This website includes news on the latest UFC fights.

UFC

http://www.ufc.com

The official UFC website features information on today's top fighters.

INDEX